By the River She Danced

Sophie Phan

Copyright © 2025 Sophie Phan

This work is copyright. Apart from any fair dealing for the purposes of private study, research, criticism or review, as permitted by the Copyright Act 1968, no part may be reproduced by any process without prior written permission. Enquiries should be addressed to the publisher.

Sophie Phan – By the River She Danced

978-1-7641269-7-7 (Paperback)

 A catalogue record for this book is available from the National Library of Ausrtralia

Cover artwork: Sophie Phan
Cover & internal design: Ronald Proft

Delphian Books
+61 2 8625 5530
www.delphianbooks.com.au
Printed in Australia

Contents

Foreword	v
Author's Note	vii
Where the Light Begins	1
Mr. Button	5
A Forgotten Story	9
The Whispering Shoes	13
By the River She Danced	17
Wednesday Night	21
Smoothie of Surprises	25
Beee Careful	29
Dancing in the Rain	31
Shakespeare in the Pantry	35
About the Author	39

This book is lovingly dedicated to the dreamers, the seekers, and the quiet souls who believe that even the smallest spark of hope can light the darkest night.

To my family, friends, and mentors who held my hand through storms and celebrated with me in sunshine, your love is the ink that fills these pages.

To the strangers whose kindness stitched my courage back together, you remind me that the world still glows with warmth.

And to every reader who opens this book, you are the final piece of this journey, turning words into meaning and stories into shared hearts. May these pages remind you that you, too, carry a story worth telling, a light worth shining, and a journey worth living.

Foreword

Stories help us understand one another by revealing the lives we have lived. In this collection, Sophie Thi Phan shares her journey, her stories, with wit, wonder, and remarkable wisdom.

She invites readers into the experiences she and her friends faced as immigrants from Vietnam, offering narratives that resonate far beyond cultural boundaries.

These are beautifully crafted, heartfelt stories — rich with lessons for anyone, whether born in Australia or elsewhere.

This is a book to be read and reread. Each time it will reveal new insights and gentle lessons that speak to and stay with you, the reader.

Mark Hunter
Author
World Champion of Public Speaking 2009

Author's Note

As you turn these pages, you may notice that while the characters and journeys are imagined, the emotions and experiences they reflect, are deeply universal.

Each story is a tapestry woven from creativity, shaped by the timeless struggles, joys and triumphs we all share as human beings. Though I craft them from imagination, they may carry echoes of reality, reminding us that in fiction we often discover shared truths.

Where the Light Begins

What does moving forward mean to you?

For me, moving forward is not always about forgetting the past. Sometimes, just sometimes, it is about learning to carry it with grace, turning emotional pain into courage, and letting each small step forward lead toward healing.

For Mai, moving forward meant more than just surviving. It meant letting go of resentment and avoiding that feeling of chasing what once felt impossible. It meant choosing to truly live.

Thirteen years ago, Mai escaped a marriage that left deep scars, not just on her skin, but on her spirit.

An Asian woman with warm eyes and a quiet determination, she had spent years enduring domestic violence in silence. One morning, with trembling hands and a five-year-old child on her hip, Mai walked out the door and never looked back. But the escape was only the beginning.

In the early years, survival was simple: working hard, providing food for her child and keeping silent to stay safe. She cleaned houses during the days and packed boxes in warehouses at nights. Her feet ached, her back hurt, but her heart, her heart learned to trust that even after darkness, the sun would rise and her life would glow with hope and joy again.

She used to believe that hard work would bring her dignity, that love would heal her if she rebuilt her life with a new husband. It was the story people around her told, that a woman's worth lies in becoming a wife again.

So Mai searched. She tried to love again. She trusted too soon, gave her heart too freely, and found herself disappointed. Misunderstood. Alone again, feeling like maybe she was the problem.

Thirteen years passed.

She created a home where her small family could feel safe and warm, where food was on the table, and every bill paid. But what was not in her new home was the happiness she sought.

"I think I'm broken," she once whispered to herself in the kitchen at 2 in the morning, staring at her reflection in a chipped teacup.

This feeling did not vanish with time. It showed up in panic attacks, sleepless nights with tears, and invisible walls she didn't know she had built. Some mornings, she couldn't breathe. Some days, she felt invisible, like a ghost in her own life. Post-traumatic stress became her shadow.

But Mai kept going.

For her child.

For the girl inside her who once believed in joy.

For the version of herself who danced barefoot in her hometown under a sky full of stars before the world became cold.

And then something changed, not suddenly, but slowly, like dawn.

It began with a walk at sunrise. A journal entry that ended with, "I want to live." A therapy session where she said, "I don't want to be afraid anymore." A quiet friend who listened. A workshop that helped her speak. A room full of women who understood.

She realized she didn't have to wait for someone to love her to feel whole. She didn't need a new partner to validate her worth. She could rebuild from within.

She learned to forgive, not to excuse the pain, but to free herself from carrying it. She practised compassion toward the woman she used to be, the one who stayed too long, hoped too much, and blamed herself too often.

She laughed again and more often. She began to dance with her child in the kitchen. She grew herbs in her windowsill. She wore bright colors and bold lipstick.

After years of silence, a beautiful afternoon light stirred something in Mai. She reached into the back of a forgotten closet and pulled out a dusty camera, one that captured her childhood dreams, now wrapped in cobwebs and doubt. Holding it, Mai wondered if her hands still remembered how to frame beauty...or if time has erased that magic.

But as she wandered through parks and quiet streets capturing moments, sunlight tangled in branches, her childlike laugh filled the air and her own shadow stretched long in the afternoon. Mai had begun to see the world differently. More importantly, she began to see herself differently.

Each photo held a quiet truth, a pain endured, and a joy rediscovered.

Instead of waiting for a gallery invitation, Mai built her own online display, a simple website titled "Light After Silence." She uploaded her photos with trembling pride, pairing each image with a caption that whispered of her journey. Slowly, people found their way to her corner of the internet. Some left comments; Others sent messages. But most people just looked and felt something.

Mai's favorite image was one she took of herself: walking forward on a misty morning, the rising sun just beginning to break through. Below it, her artist's note read:

"I used to believe healing meant hiding what hurt. But through the lens, I've learned to hold it gently, frame it honestly, and let it speak.

The light I searched for was never lost.

I've carried it within me all along.

And this…

is where I begin."

To everyone who has ever carried pain, heartbreak, or the weight of silence, this message is for you. You are not broken. You are becoming. And the light? It's not at the end of the tunnel. It begins wherever and whenever you choose to rise.

Mr. Button

Dear Diary,

Let me tell you about my best friend, Button. His name alone tells you he is not your average guy. This man has the power to both activate my dreams and drive me completely bonkers at the same time.

Have you ever met someone like Button? If you haven't met one, let me share mine.

Button was the kind of guy who was always in control of everything, except his impulse to mess with me. This, he did not always control. He has this weird way of inspiring me to chase my dreams but also making me feel like I was a real actor in his main storyline. I remember when I told him about my big ambition to become a professional dancer. Was I serious? Not really. Did Button take it seriously? Oh, absolutely.

So, he dragged me to this salsa class, telling me, "This is it, buddy. This is how you start. I'll teach you the basics, and you'll be on your way to greatness."

Now, here is the thing: Button can dance. I mean, this guy had rhythm in his bones. Me? My dancing skills were somewhere between "awkward uncle at a wedding" and "person being chased by bees." But that did not stop him from enthusiastically taking me under his wing.

We stepped onto the dance floor, and he immediately took over, moving gracefully, spinning me around, teaching me the steps.

"Just follow my lead," he said. Easy for him to say. I looked like a confused octopus trying to salsa. But Button? No. He glided around, making it look effortless. The worst part? Well, Button started dancing with the other ladies in the class. One by one, he twirled them around, flashing them that 'Button' smile which he used to charm the universe.

Meanwhile, I was there, awkwardly standing in the corner, pretending not to mind that my best friend was waltzing through my life while I was struggling to figure out where my feet went. He gave me a thumbs-up from across the room like, "You're doing great, buddy!" Yeah, sure, if "great" means "barely surviving."

But at the end of the night, it was always Button and I, sitting on a curb somewhere, talking about life and all its weird twists and turns.

You know Diary, on another beautiful day, I had another one of those "only-with-Button" days. I swear, that guy must have fallen straight out of a UFO and landed right into my life. Button insisted he was an alien, and honestly, I sometimes believed him. It was the only explanation for how he flipped personalities faster than I could change a Netflix show!

I learned so much from him.

First of all, he taught me to actually talk about my feelings. And trust me, that was no small feat for someone who usually preferred bottling things up like a good vintage wine. With Button, you could not really hide your feeling because he had this eerie ability to sniff them out. It was like he knew when something was up even before I did. He would just stare and say, "So, what's bothering you, buddy?" And the next thing I knew, I was spilling my guts.

And he was the guy who worked like no human I had ever seen. He was determined, driven, and his definition of "working late" put me to shame. While I was deep in a Netflix binge by 10 p.m., he was still up at 2 a.m. solving the world's problems or, at least, our tech issues. Seriously, he did not rest until he figured out a solution. It was impressive... and, well, kind of worrying. I sometimes wondered if he ever just relaxed.

However, for all the times Button drove me up the wall, there were moments when he really came through. Like the time I was going through a rough patch. Work was a mess, life was chaotic, and I felt like giving up on everything. That was when Button showed up at my door with his big belly, a pizza, and his signature pep talk: "Look Buddy, life's like a dance. Sometimes you're leading, sometimes you're just stepping on toes. But either way, you keep moving."

And somehow, it worked. He always knew how to lift me up, even after he teased me a hundred times. He had this knack for making me feel like I could do anything, even after he had just finished saying, "Hey Sophie, you're still in the learning process."

So yeah, Button was an absolute enigma. Alien or not, he was one of the kindest, strangest friends I could ever ask for.

He was also the guy who inspired me, supported me, and believed in me more than anyone else. He was a whirlwind of contradictions, but at the end of the day, he was my best friend, and I would not trade him for anything.

Do you have a friend like this? Please let me know.

A Forgotten Story

When Minh stepped off the plane in Sydney, Australia, he expected a land of golden beaches, friendly kangaroos, and an exciting new life. What he didn't expect was the suffocating heat, the overwhelming scent of meat pies at the airport, and his friend showing a work uniform before he even said his first 'G'day to a local or set foot on Australia's sunlit beaches.

"Tomorrow, 8 A.M. Nail salon. No excuses."

That was his grand welcome. No fancy Australian barbecue. No "Welcome to your new life!" Just a polyester uniform and the strong scent of acetone in his future.

The nail salon was an entirely different universe. Women chatted nonstop, showing off pictures of their latest cats, kids, and celebrity nail inspirations.

Minh, meanwhile, sat in the back, scrubbing foot basins and wondering how his life had gone from dreams of becoming an artist to scraping dead skin off strangers' feet.

His manager ran the place like a military base.

"Minh, faster!"

"Minh, don't talk back!"

"Minh, no customer wants to hear about your dreams; just do the nails and smile!"

His hands were covered in glitter and polish, but inside, Minh's heart felt colorless.

Late at night, when the salon was finally quiet, Minh pulled out his sketchbook. His fingers ached from filing nails all day, but his mind was still full of ideas. He wanted to be an artist, to design, to create something bigger than just perfect French tips.

One quiet night, as the world outside slowed to a hush, Minh's workmate, Huong caught a glimpse of him sketching in the corner of the nail shop.

His pencil danced wildly across the page, breathing life into a new idea, drawing of a sun rising over Sydney's skyline, symbolizing hope, new beginnings, and dreams yet to unfold.

"Why are you wasting time? You have had a good job. Why are you still thinking about drawing?"

Minh sighed. "Because I love it."

Huong rolled her eyes. "Loving something doesn't pay the bills."

Maybe she was right. Maybe Minh should just accept his fate, follow his relatives' expectations, and let go of his silly dream.

Like many immigrants chasing a better tomorrow, Minh arrived in Sydney with nothing but hope in his heart and dreams in his eyes. Young and full of energy, with his broken English, he rolled up his sleeves, ready to shape his dreams with the strength of his own hands, whether at a bustling nail salon, a warm-smelling bakery, the golden fields of a farm, or the hum of a factory line.

Each drop of sweat whispered a promise to his future self. Through hard work and quiet resilience, he stitched together a new beginning.

In every calloused hand and tired smile, Minh carried the fire of hope, refusing to let go of his dream of drawing and art.

Every night back home after work, Minh used to fill notebooks with sketches of landscapes, faces, and abstract designs. But in Australian, the daylight hours left no room for dreams, only for hard work and silent determination. Art would probably not pay the bills.

Day by day, despite of the struggles, loneliness, and exhaustion, Minh held on to a small flame of hope deep inside.

One night, as Minh sat sketching in an old notebook, his roommate saw his work and said. "Minh, this is amazing. You should share your work."

Minh hesitated and decided to upload a few drawings on social media. He didn't expect anything, but within days, people started noticing. A local café reached out, asking if they could display his art. Then, a small art competition caught his eye.

With trembling hands, Minh submitted his work. Days later, he received an email. He had won a third place. It wasn't first, but it was something. A spark. A beginning. A dream.

For the first time in a long time, Minh felt like his dreams weren't so distant. He continued working at the salon, polishing nails to pay for his new night class, studying art. Every free moment, Minh spent drawing, creating, and pushing himself forward. It wasn't easy. There were still struggles, still expectations weighing him down. But now, Minh had something that kept him going.

Hope.

Life is sometimes complicated. People may think they know what's best for you. You may face struggles that make you want to give up. But dreams do not disappear just because others don't believe in them.

Hold on to hope. Never let go of your dreams, for one day, the dream you quietly nurture could become the spark that lights someone else's way.

That one day, your forgotten story might just become the one that people remember.

Minh – A forgotten story *(Image Artist: Sophie Phan)*

The Whispering Shoes

Can you tell a lot about a person by their shoes? What about Lien's shoes? They scream, "Watch me! I've survived five summers, three floods, and one scooter accident." They were white, well, they used to be.

Lien, an Asian overseas student, bought her beautiful white Oxford shoes at the Sydney night market for a cheap $12.

They were two sizes too tight, made her feet sweat like noodles in hot soup, and squeaked every time she moved. But she loved them. They were her lucky shoes, even though the left one was slowly falling apart like a secret unraveling in whispered pieces.

So, on the night of her very first real date, with a Western guy, she wore them.

His name was Alex, from Netherlands. He was tall with blue eyes, and a smile like a movie actor who had too many teeth. Lien met him at EF International Language School in Chippendale Sydney, where she accidentally told him she loved hamsters, when she actually meant hamburgers. Even though Alex laughed for five minutes, he still asked for her phone number.

Lien had wanted to look cute, elegant, and smart on the first date. So she curled her short black hair (bad idea), wore her flowery dress (itchy), and put on her favourite white Oxford shoes. She told herself, "Lien, you are a strong, confident Asian girl. Let's meet Alex."

Everything was okay until Lien reached Central train station.

Just as she stepped onto the platform, flap! The left shoe opened like a broken wallet. Flap-squeak, flap-squeak. Every step sounded like a duck walking on bubble wrap.

When Lien arrived at the cafe on George Street, Sydney, she dragged her half-dead shoe behind her like a small child refusing to go to school. And then she saw him. Alex.

He was leaning by the entrance of the cafeteria, looking like he had just stepped out of a travel magazine.

He was wearing a casual button-up blue shirt and smiling like he just won a free holiday. Lien, on the other hand, looked like a panicked flamingo.

"Hey, Lien!" he said.

"Hi!" Lien tried to act naturally as she walked up to Alex, her heart racing beneath her calm smile. With each step, her shoes tapped the floor with a gentle click-clack, like the soft rhythm of a marimba, light, playful, and just a little too loud in the quiet air between them. It was as if her footsteps carried a melody of nerves and anticipation, dancing closer to the one who unknowingly made her heart sing.

He tilted his head. "You're… making music already?"

Lien laughed. "Yes, my shoes… they are… making a happy noise."

He smiled. "That's a nice soundtrack."

They sat down, and that's when the romantic moments almost died.

Lien pulled her chair in—PPPPFFFT!

A sound escaped from that chair that no one could ignore. You know the one.

They both froze.

Lien's face turned as red as a chili pepper.

Alex raised an eyebrow.

Lien whispered, "It was the chair. Not me. I promise."

Alex laughed. A big, warm laugh showing all his teeth.

Lien tried to hide her shame by drinking water. Well, that was a bad idea. Her elbow hit the jug and SPLASH! Water went all over her face. Now Lien looked like a nervous jellyfish.

Alex handed her a napkin. "You okay?"

"Yes. I like... staying hydrated," Lien said, trying to joke. Alex laughed again.

"Oh, this boy laughed at everything." Lien liked him.

Then, Lien tried to cross her legs, and disaster struck again. Her left shoe said goodbye, flew across the floor, bounced under the table, and landed near the barista's foot.

They both stared at it.

"Oh, my shoe. My dreams. All over the floor," Lien stammered.

Alex looked at her and said, "Is this part of your escape plan?"

Lien covered her face. "I'm not normally this fast, Alex!"

Alex laughed so hard he snorted. "Lien, this is the best date I've ever had."

Lien retrieved her shoe with all the grace of a baby deer. She slipped it back on and decided, if she could survive this night, she could survive anything.

The rest of the date? Wonderful.

Alex and Lien talked about their countries, languages, food, and how he once, in a sushi restaurant, mistook wasabi for avocado and cried. Lien told him how she once practised English by talking to her neighbor's cat. Alex didn't judge. He just smiled like Lien was the most interesting girl in the world.

He walked Lien to Central train station afterward. Her shoe squeaked the whole way like a tiny duck cheering them on.

Before she stepped onto the train, Alex said, "You know, most people try to be perfect. You just showed up as yourself. That's... rare. I really like that."

Lien smiled so hard, her cheeks hurt. "Even with crazy shoes?"

"Especially with crazy shoes," he said.

They didn't kiss that night. But Alex asked to meet Lien again.

And next time?

Lien wore the same white Oxford shoes.

Because sometimes, when things go wrong, they actually go wonderfully well, right?

By the River She Danced

So here we are.

The dance floor at Cabra-Vale Diggers shimmered under the kaleidoscope of lights, gold, blue, violet, and soft reds swirled across the polished wood like dreams floating in motion. The DJ spun a familiar song, and with the first nostalgic hum of "By the Rivers of Babylon", time slowed.

Kim stepped onto the floor, her silver shoes catching the lights like stars. Her hands gently floated to her sides, and her body began to move, slow, thoughtful, graceful. She was dancing alone, but her presence filled the space like a story unfolding without words.

As the melody filled the room, it took her back, not just years, but lifetimes.

The guitar's gentle hum became a vessel, carrying her through layers of time, through memories folded deep within her soul.

And suddenly, she was there.

Vietnam.

Fifty years ago.

The scent of warm earth.

The tiny hand clutched in hers.

The screams of urgency during a dark night and the clatter of sandals as she was pulled away, put on a boat, her heart breaking into pieces as if she could never mend. Her ten-year-old child waved from the dock, crying, while she whispered a silent prayer to the wind, "One day son, I'll come back for you. One day."

That day did not come for years.

The waves of the ocean were not just water, they were fear, hunger, sickness, and death. Days blurred into nights on that boat with strangers who wept and held each other in silence. When the boat finally landed, it was not freedom waiting, it was a crowded refugee camp in Malaysia, where the only constant was uncertainty. Time lost meaning there. They counted the days not by sunrise, but by meals, roll calls and the letters that never came.

When Kim finally arrived in Australia, her soul was worn thin, but her hope still flickered. She did not speak the language. She could not read the road signs or understand the questions. But she could scrub. She could wash. She worked in a kitchen, washing dishes, hands deep in suds while others laughed around her, their voices an orchestra she could not join.

Later, she packed chicken in a freezing poultry factory at night for a living. By day, she nursed her two more babies, their giggles the music of her tired heart. Then came the job at a sewing factory, needle after needle, garment after garment, as her fingers stitched clothes for others while she quietly stitched together her dreams. "One day," she still whispered, "I will speak English. I will tell my story."

And for a while, one of the dreams looked real for her. Kim saved money for her dream home. She and her husband bought a house. Her children grew. Laughter returned to her dinner table. She was proud, proud of her sacrifices, proud of her family, proud of what her hands had built.

However, rainbow skies sometimes turn grey without warning.

Their dream business of sewing factory failed. The house had to be sold.

One day, her husband came home with a young woman on his arm, a child at his side. "This is my new family," he said, as if those words weren't knives. Her knees gave way. Her heart did not break, it shattered, again.

What followed was not just a divorce, it was a quiet collapse of all she had carried for decades.

Her dream of learning and speaking English vanished under the weight of bills and fatigue. Her body, once strong, fell ill. Depression visited like an uninvited guest and refused to leave. Some nights, she could not speak at all.

It was a time when her children became her voice. They translated her letters, fixed the Internet, sat with her at the doctor appointments. They became the light in her long tunnel, the branches she reached for when drowning.

But tonight, tonight she danced.

Back to Cabra-Vale Diggers, as the haunting melody swirled through the room, the music wrapped around Kim like an old embrace. Kim's hips moved in slow swing motion. Her arms waved gently like reeds by a river, her eyes half-closed, remembering. Not in sorrow, but in resilience and courage.

The other dancers faded. She was not performing. She was remembering. Honouring.

Her breath steadied. Her back straightened. The lights spun around her like ghosts of all the lives she had lived and let go of. Her feet whispered across the floor:

I survived.

I endured.

I loved.

I lost.

And yet, I am still here.

As the final notes played and the song faded into silence, Kim slowed her steps and stopped in the centre of the floor. There was no applause, but she did not need it. Her dance was not for show.

A moment later, someone walked over, an older man with a soft smile, and asked gently, "Would you like to dance?"

Kim smiled. A quiet, peaceful smile. She nodded.

She knew now: she did not need to speak perfect English to tell her story.

She had already spoken it.

Through her silence. Through her movement.

Through the dance of a life lived with quiet courage.

Wednesday Night

Come and sit with me for a moment, and I'll share with you a glimpse of Lily's world.

Lily is an Asian girl, quiet and thoughtful, learning to shape her voice at a community club. Though she often feels small and overlooked, Lily is beginning to discover that even the softest voice can carry strength, and even the most fragile flower can stand tall in the strong wind and storm.

After the weight of a long, tiring day, Lily finds herself sitting in a quiet corner of her bedroom, soaking up the kind of stillness that comes only after a storm.

Outside, yet another storm. The wind again howls like a wild creature, fierce and untamed, and it rattles the windows with a relentless energy. In its fierce gusts, she imagines a dandelion, so delicate yet resilient, swaying in the storm, its tiny seeds clinging desperately, waiting for that brief, blessed moment of calm.

She whispers to herself, "That's me… small, fragile… but still holding on."

In many ways, Lily feels like that dandelion. Something small and unseen, left to grow on the edges of the road, feeling weak and out of place, but holding on with quiet determination through its storms, her storms.

Life has often made her feel misplaced and unworthy, set apart by struggles and obstacles that have marked her path. But even a weed has roots that run deep, roots that know how to hold on when the world seems determined to tear it down.

At the community club, where she practices her public speaking skills, Lily has learned how quickly voices can be silenced. When someone interrupts her, dismisses her, or laughs at her accent, the words in her throat tremble. More than once, she has walked home thinking, "Why can't they see I'm trying to make them happy?"

Tonight, as she sits in her quiet corner, the storm reminds her of those challenges. So often, she deals with people who see only what they want to see, who label her as weak simply because she is different from what they expect.

It hurts when people cannot see past their judgments to the heart that beats beneath the surface. Sometimes, Lily feels like her own hopes and dreams are pushed aside, buried under the shadow of others' expectations. Alone in her room, she admits softly, "I'm not invisible. I just… haven't found the right way to shine yet."

Yet here she is, still holding on. There is a fire in her, small but fierce, that refuses to be extinguished, no matter how hard the winds blow.

Even in the middle of being needled, blamed, and pushed around in a volunteering club that sometimes feels more like a circus of critics than a community, Lily has learned to carve out tiny moments of peace just for herself. Yes, it is bewildering when people who should simply do their jobs toss their responsibilities aside and treat her struggles like they are unnoticed, or cruel entertainment.

Once, when someone sneered, she wanted to reply, "Is my worth measured only by your gaze?" But the words stayed locked in her chest.

Instead, she smiled quietly and thought, "One day, I'll stand tall enough to answer you with my strength."

And somehow, through it all, she has found ways to survive, to smile more often, and to bring light into her life, even if it is just a single flicker in a sea of shadows.

Here lies the heart of Lily's quiet arc: the girl, who once shrank beneath harsh words, is learning to meet them with her own kind of courage. Every storm she endures becomes part of her training, and teaching her how to stand.

As the wind continues to rage outside, Lily closes her eyes and makes a wish. "Please... let tomorrow be kinder. Let me be braver." She wishes that dawn will bring a softer breeze, a brighter sky, and a little less of the storm that surrounds her. She hopes the fierce winds that blew so hard today will carry away some of the weariness from her heart, making room for a fresh start, for peace, and for the strength to keep going.

Tomorrow, she hopes, will bloom with a new kind of light, one that she can hold onto as she navigates this path.

In these quiet moments, sitting alone in the darkness, Lily realizes that there is a beauty in her resilience. No matter how many times she has been trampled on or pushed aside, she keeps getting back up, like that dandelion swaying in the storm. She may be small, but she is determined.

"One day," she whispers, "I'll bloom in my own time, in my own way."

So tonight, Lily holds onto her wish for a brighter tomorrow, one filled with hope and light, where she can live truly as herself, unburdened by others' judgments. Like the dandelion, she'll keep growing, finding her way through the toughest of soils.

Lily is not just surviving; she is lighting up her own life, bit by bit, choosing to bloom even when the world tells her she is just a weed. And tomorrow, with any luck, she'll stand a little taller, a little stronger, and a little closer to the life she deserves.

Like Lily, we all face storms and moments when we are blamed, dismissed, or made to feel small.

But let us choose to rise above those judgments. Let us choose to speak when our voice longs to be heard. Even the most fragile flower can stand tall in the strong wind and storm. So let us rise, and bloom together, and shine in our own light.

Wednesday night. 10th October 2024. Burwood NSW.

Smoothie of Surprises

*I*f life were a receipe, Han added the strangest ingredients.

Han was an Asian finance student, who discovered his true passion in a most unexpected place.

He entered Australia like a potato rolling in a fruit salad, slightly confused by bright lights, obviously out of place with endless announcements, and a sea of strangers who were too busy to notice a guy like Han holding a backpack, a dream, and absolutely having no idea which way to walk.

No welcome committee, no dramatic hugs, just Han, a trolley with a wobbly wheel, and a burning question: "Did I just land in my future… or a food court?"

Han clutched his single suitcase, filled with two pairs of jeans, a secondhand rice cooker, and a couple of spring rolls wrapped tightly in banana leaves.

Han had a clear mission, to get a finance degree, land a six-figure job, and give his parents the life they sacrificed everything for.

His father had spent three decades fixing motorcycles in the humid corners of Hanoi. His mother, a high school teacher, had sewn clothes at night to save for Han's tuition. They had placed their dreams in his hands, like a fragile porcelain bowl.

But something was not quite right.

Every lecture for Han felt like a mild coma. Charts and spreadsheets blurred before his eyes. While his classmates debated investment portfolios, Han found himself daydreaming about dough. Not a metaphorical "dough", it was literal dough. Bread. Pastry. Flaky, buttery croissants whispering his name in French.

This obsession began when he took a part-time job at a local bakery called "Rise & Shine" in Campsie. He meant to stay just a month, you know, for rent. But one morning, while watching sourdough rise in the oven like a sun of hope, Han felt something stir in his soul… and stomach.

He started experimenting, not with finance models, but with flour, yeast, and flavors. At home, his tiny student kitchen became a lab of joy and occasional small fires. He tried adding lemongrass to banana bread. He stuffed croissants with durian. He even invented something he called the "pho-gelato roll." (It did not go viral, thankfully.)

One day, disaster struck.

The bakery manager called in sick, and Han, the casual shift worker with flour in his hair and confidence in his shoes, was left alone to open the store.

He panicked.

Customers arrived expecting buttery perfection. Han had only slept three hours and could not remember which button started the espresso machine. In his sleepy daze, he accidentally mixed up coffee orders, and over-baked half the batch of apple turnovers. And in a final act of desperation, he created a "breakfast smoothie" from leftover lemons, sweet chili sauce, mango yogurt, and a little bit of regret.

He handed it to the customer with a straight face.

"Here is our new… Lemon-chili sunrise smoothie," he said.

The customer took a sip. Paused. Then said, "It is weird... but I like it. It kicks you in the face, in a good way."

Han blinked his eyes. "Thanks... I think?"

Somehow, it caught on. People came back. Not for the smoothie, that was never repeated, but for Han's energy, creativity, and chaotic charm.

And something clicked inside him.

Maybe, he thought, this was it. Not finance. Not numbers. But bakery flavors. People. The smell of fresh bread in the morning. The simple joy of making something from scratch.

When he told his parents he was quitting finance to pursue baking full-time, his mother screamed so loudly that the neighbor's dog cried. His father did not speak for two days. But then, quietly, his dad messaged him: "Follow what makes you wake up early. Just... do not burn the house down."

So Han went all in. He enrolled in a pastry course. He got up at 4 a.m. everyday.

Han kneaded dough with his hands and more than a handful of hope, waking before the sun to press through fatigue and flour.

He whisked eggs and dreams together, watching mixtures rise, collapse, and sometimes surprise him.

He folded pastry sheets with patience, even when his heart felt heavy with doubt.

He failed, burned batches, mixed up recipes, dropped trays, and stood there, silent, feeling the sting of disappointment settle on his apron.

He cried in quiet corners of the kitchen, tears mixing with the steam of determination.

But he tried again, every single morning, because something deep inside him refused to give up.

He was not just learning how to bake…

He was learning how to become.

Five years later, Han opened his own bakery "Lemon Life" in Cabramatta, a tribute to that chaotic, beautiful morning of weird smoothies and unexpected beginnings.

Today, the shop is filled with laughter, music, and smells that make people nostalgic for childhoods they never had. Han greets everyone with the same line: "Life gives you lemons? Add butter and flour, a hint of sugar, bake, and serve warm".

Han is not rich, not in finance terms. But he is full. Of joy. Of friends. Of stories.

And occasionally… of lemon smoothie memories.

So, follow your heart. Even if it leads you to a bakery full of burnt croissants and chili smoothies, because that might just be where your joy is waiting, and the who you want to become.

Beee Careful

It begins with a moment I never would have expected.

I am sitting next to the swimming pool at a Sydney resort. Sitting all peaceful in a dappled sunlight under an umbrella.

I am wearing my new blue swimming suit, sipping a Coke and thinking to myself, "Yeah, life isn't so bad." I lay here, stretching my legs out and closing my eyes.

Pretty nice thought, eh isn't it?

Then, I feel this weird tingling sensation. Something is crawling on my head. I reach up to scratch it. Oh my gosh, it's a bee!

I try not to freak out as I flick him off me. He lands right in my Coke. I stare at him for a few seconds. He seems to be having a few sips. I use my straw to carefully pick him up and out.

Now what? I could put him on the floor and crush him with my magazine. Hmmm. No. I think I will let this little guy live.

In my culture, bees are lucky! I once had a bee hive in the corner of my ceiling. My friend told me, "Don't remove it. Leave it there and you will be rich!"

I did leave it. I have been waiting for several years, but nothing happens.

I haven't been rich yet.

Do you know that bees are attracted to the color blue? They see ultraviolet light. It helps them find and identify the flowers that they pollinate. Bees can't see red color at all.

I gently place a straw, with the bee on the ground and he climbs off. I feel happy. A bee's stinger has a tiny barb, like a fish hook. When they sting someone, it gets stuck. The bee tries to get away but damages itself.

Ouch! He stings me. I grab him off me, and he falls to the ground.

I look down. My bee is laying there, struggling a bit. After about a minute, he stops moving.

My head hurts a little. I don't know what to do.

Ah, I know what to do. I order a cocktail from a waiter. It's called a "Bee's Knees" cocktail. It is made with gin, some honey and lemon juice.

I really feel bad that the little guy has died. He was only "beeeing" himself

My drink arrives and I take a big sip. I stretch my legs out, close my eyes and try to relax.

Next time, I will wear a red swimming suit.

Dancing in the Rain

*E*very dawn writes a new page, but today, the rain wants to write its own story.

Ann had grown accustomed to the silence of her old apartment. No laughter echoed through the halls, no voices called her name. Her relatives and previous family, consumed by their own lives and indifferent to her, long since drifted away.

Ann knew the feeling of their absence, the empty seats at the table, and the birthday cards that never came. Regardless of all of these moments of indifference, Ann had decided that she wouldn't let their neglect define her.

Every morning, she woke up with the sun, her spirit unbroken by the lack of warmth. Ann found joy in the little things, her morning coffee, the chirping of birds outside the window, and the vibrant colors of the town as it came to life.

Her job at the local retail book store at Bondi was her sanctuary. Surrounded by wonderful and great people, along with the intimacy of many books, Ann felt connected to the world in a way her previous family had never understood.

Ann also found joy watching the rain, finding solace in its rhythmic dance. But this year, the rain held a bittersweet melody for her. It has been a year since Ann's mother passed away, a year filled with heartache and regret.

Ann's ex-partner, a lovely man who believed that empathy was a luxury he could not afford, would repeatedly say it was not a good idea for her to visit her mom overseas. Ann missed her mom dying. She missed saying goodbye. She missed holding her mom's hands one last time.

Recently, one evening, as the sky darkened and the first drops of rain began to fall, Ann stepped outside. The local town, usually bustling with life, was empty. She stood in the middle, feeling the cool rain kiss her skin. As the storm intensified, Ann closed my eyes, letting the rain wash over her.

In the distance, Ann heard the soft hum of a familiar tune. It was her mother's lullaby, carried by the wind and the rain. Tears mingled with the raindrops on her cheeks as she opened my eyes. There, in the heart of the storm, Ann saw a figure. It was her mother, smiling warmly, her form shimmering like a ghost.

Her mother's voice echoed through the rain, "Life is not about waiting for the storm to pass, it's about learning to dance in the rain."*

Ann's mother had shared those words during a difficult time, before she passed away, and I finally understood their depth. Life's storms were inevitable, but Ann could choose how to face them, like choosing to face her fears, her challenges, maybe even her loneliness.

Ann began to dance. She twirled and danced on the wet pavement, her clothes soaked and her hair plastered to her face.

The rain, a reminder of her sorrow, now felt like a blessing. Each rain drop, each twirl, was a tribute to her mother's memory, now a celebration of life and resilience.

In that moment, Ann understood that love didn't have to come from her previous broken family or relatives. It could be found in the kindness of strangers, the warmth of a well-loved book, and the simple beauty of a rainy afternoon.

Ladies and gentlemen.

At that time, Ann knew she didn't need a love life to love life. She didn't need to wait for a better day. She learned to dance in the rain, to find beauty in the storm, and to cherish every drop of her existence.

Ann knew that there would be more storms to come, but she was no longer afraid.

Ann's apartment might have been silent, but her life was filled with music, the music of her own making. Ann loved life not despite the lack of love, or relative connection, but because she learned to love herself and the world around her.

And as she danced in the rain, she knew exactly where she was meant to be.

***Note:** "Life is not about waiting for the storm to pass, it's about learning to dance in the rain." Quote by Vivian Greene

Shakespeare in the Pantry

It begins with a call in the dark early morning.

My phone rings for the third time. It's 3 a.m. My heart thumps. Who calls me at this early time?

"This is a police officer, calling from Vietnam. Your aunt Kim has died. We need your consent to investigate the cause of her death. Do you give us permission to autopsy her body?"

"Oh no, are you serious? What are you talking about? I just spoke to her on the phone yesterday!"

"Do we have your consent?"

My Aunt Kim was a beautiful kind person who took very good care of her family. She was old school, and strict. Set in her ways and too caring.

Aunt Kim's mother died when Kim was seventeen years old. Her father moved out with a new wife shortly after, forcing Kim to quit school and get a job to support her eight younger siblings.

She worked so hard, but they often struggled to have enough food. In her older years, Kim was a food hoarder. She stocked foods, all types of foods, dried food, tinned foods, junk foods.

Her pantry and her wardrobe were always over full of foods, such as tuna, baked beans, tomato, beetroot, noodles, rice…

After the Vietnam war, the United Nations would parachute airdrop lots of tinned food to people. It seemed like Kim was worried that it might happen again. She probably kept cash under her mattress.

In Aunt Kim's bedroom she stored piles of beautiful dishes still in their packaging. Her bedroom wardrobe was full of expensive pots and pans. They were all unopened and she would never ever use them. What was she waiting for?

Aunt Kim worked all day. So when I was ten years old, I cooked the meals for our family.

Aunt Kim's pantry was unlike any other. On one shelf, Shakespeare's Hamlet sat sulking beside cans of sardines. Romeo and Juliet leaned dramatically against a tower of baked beans, as if love itself depended on legumes.

The noodles looked jealous, and the rice just kept quiet in the corner, next to Shakespeare's Macbeth. Who needed a library card when you could check out a sonnet while reaching for tomato soup?

We both loved reading books. Aunt Kim never learned to read English very well, but she was proud of her big "pantry library" and complete works of Shakespeare. And me? I learned to read English while standing on a stool, balancing a can of tuna in one hand and holding a Shakespeare play in the other hand. Who said you could not get your daily serving of drama along with your dinner?

Shakespeare said, "Expectation is the root of all heartache."

I lived with my Aunt Kim when I was young, instead of my parents.

When I was seven years old, Kim owned a shop in the ground floor of a high-rise shopping centre. I used to play in the back room of the shop while they worked.

One day a loud siren went off while I was playing. Smoke poured in. People started shouting, a terrible fire started on the upper storey of the building. People were in panic and running for their lives.

My aunt shouted at me, "Run Sophie. This is fire ... danger!"

But I just stood there. Frozen. The more she yelled at me to come, the more I froze. It was like my body was not mine. I could not move, the fear was too much. Suddenly my uncle grabbed me and swung me up into his arms.

We rushed from the building, while above us, desperate people jumped from the top floor that day to their deaths.

Desperate people jumped from the top floor that day to their death. Sixty people died that day in Ho Chi Minh City – The International Trading Centre Fire, in the year 2004.

I have not entered into any shopping centre since that day.

Several years later, I went back to Vietnam. I ran into one of my aunt's friends. His eyes flew open, "Sophie!!! You're dead already! ... How are you here?" He thought I had died in the fire. Apparently, I was a ghost wandering around Ho Chi Minh City.

Being the eldest daughter, and eldest niece, came with... well, expectations. "Sophie, you're not good enough." "Sophie, you're the problem."

I wanted to ask them, "Excuse me? I've lived abroad for more than 30 years by myself, what more do you want, a Nobel Prize?"

But instead, I swallowed it. Their words silenced me until I became almost mute.

Aunt Kim, too, was weighed down by expectations. After caring for her siblings for 30 years, she finally returned to university at the age of 50. Her brother called her crazy, but she finished her degree and became a physiotherapist. I was so proud of her. But even then, she spent all her money buying gifts for her rich siblings.

"Hey aunty," I told her once, "leave them alone. Care for yourself! Buy the gift for you. Take a holiday!"

She snapped back, "Who are you to lecture me, little kid? Shut up!"

So I smiled, took a breath, and said: "Look at me, aunty. I'm not waiting until 60 to start living. I travel. I live. I choose me."

It took me ten years, but I meant it.

"To be, or not to be, that is the question." I choose to be me.

Back to the phone call at 3 a.m.

"Sophie, are you there?" The police officer's voice breaks through my frozen silence. "Kim fell at her clinic, and stopped breathing."

"Sophie, the autopsy? Can you hear me?"

I say nothing. I am frozen, just like in that fire years ago.

Finally, I whisper, "No. Let her rest."

Covid lockdown stole my chance to meet her in her final years.

Kim was more than my aunt. She was likely my mother. She took care of me since I was five years old.

I love you mum, for the person you are. Your mission on earth is completed. You don't need to change a thing.

And as for me? Yes, I inherit some of her character traits, being kind, too kind, independent, caring, too caring, and a little feisty.

But don't worry, mum, I promise that I will never keep my books and sardines in the same pantry.

---

* Story was shared with the community at Generation Women, Sydney. August 2023

About the Author

Sophie is a dreamer, a doer, and a storyteller at heart. Once reserved, she is now more like a social butterfly, flitting gracefully from one adventure to the next.

Whether she's aiming for the bullseye in archery, experimenting with bold flavors in the kitchen, or twirling across the dance floor, Sophie lives with a spark that turns everyday moments into stories worth telling.

Her world is a colorful canvas, sometimes painted with laughter, sometimes with lessons and experiences, but always with passion. She believes in growth through challenges, joy through connection, and magic through creativity.

From chasing adventures outdoors to bringing warmth into every room she enters, Sophie is not just living life; she is dancing with it, one vibrant step at a time.

www.ingramcontent.com/pod-product-compliance
Lightning Source LLC
Chambersburg PA
CBHW061732070526
44583CB00024B/3106